A New True Book

ROCKS AND MINERALS

By Illa Podendorf

*This "true book" was prepared
under the direction of
Illa Podendorf,
formerly with the Laboratory School,
University of Chicago*

CHILDRENS PRESS, CHICAGO

Chiricahua National Monument

PHOTO CREDITS
Lynn M. Stone—2, 7, 16 (left), 19 (right), 35 (top)
James M. Mejuto—4
Julie O'Neil—6, 11
Allan Roberts—8, 10, 13 (right), 16 (right), 19 (left), 23, 27, 32, 33
James P. Rowan—13 (left), 38
Reinhard Brucker—14, 18, 21, 31, 35 (bottom), 36, 43 (right), 45
Joseph A. DiChello, Jr.—24
David Glazewski—29, 30
M. Cole—Cover, 43 (left)
Bill Thomas—37   COVER—Rock Formations, Arches National Park

Library of Congress Cataloging in Publication Data

Podendorf, Illa.
   Rocks and minerals.

   (A New true book)
   Revised edition of: The true book of rocks
and minerals. 1958.
   Summary: An introduction to the formation and
identification of a variety of rocks and
minerals.
   1. Rocks—Juvenile literature. 2. Mineralogy
—Juvenile literature. [1. Rocks. 2. Miner-
alogy] I. Title.
QE432.2.P6   1982   552   81-38494
ISBN 0-516-01648-2   AACR2

TABLE OF CONTENTS

"Spirit Mountain" of the Mohave Indians

ROCKS ARE BIG AND LITTLE

Some rocks are as big as pumpkins. Some rocks are bigger than a man.

Big rocks are called boulders.

Beach rocks, Boston Harbor

Some rocks are as small
as eggs. Some rocks are
as small as marbles.
Small rocks are broken
from big rocks.

Some rocks are rough.
Rough rocks may be
made smooth by rolling
around on the ground
among other rocks.

Rough rocks may be
made smooth by rolling
around for a long time in
water, too.

Beach in New Brunswick

Granite Mountains, Grand Teton National Park

Granite is one kind of rock. Not all granite is the same color.

All granite is alike in some ways. It is all made in the same way. It is hard. It all has crystals of quartz in it.

SOME ROCKS
ARE MADE BY FIRE

Fire-made rocks are called igneous rocks. Granite is a kind of fire-made rock. It is always made under the ground. It is a good building stone because it is very hard.

Basalt columns, Yellowstone National Park

These rocks were made
by fire. They were made
under the ground. In some
ways they are like granite.
They are different because
they have something
different in them.

Not all fire-made rocks are made under the ground. Some fire-made rocks are made from melted rock that is forced out of a volcano. This melted rock cools quickly.

Volcanic rock in Hawaii

Even the foam from the melted rock cools and forms rocks. Rocks made from foam do not weigh much.

Pumice is a rock that is made from foam. It does not weigh much. It has air spaces in it. It will float on water.

Pumice is sometimes used to polish other rocks.

Above: Pumice
Left: Tuff cone and tuff beds,
      Koko Crater, Hawaii

Some melted rock hardens into a rock that is called volcanic tuff.

Volcanic tuff is heavier than pumice. It will not float.

Obsidian

Obsidian comes from volcanoes, too. This rock is sometimes called volcanic glass. It is shiny and has sharp edges.

Basalt rocks are igneous rocks. Great walls are made of basalt rocks.

SOME ROCKS ARE MADE UNDERWATER

Some kinds of rocks are not made from melted rock.

They are made underwater. They are made from small pieces of shell and sand. Scientists call these rocks sedimentary rocks.

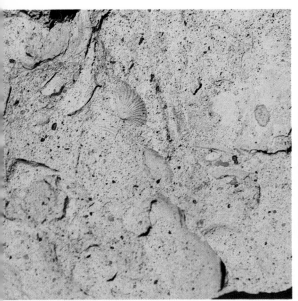
Shells in limestone

Limestone

Limestone is a
sedimentary rock that is
made underwater.
It is easy to see shells
in some pieces of limestone.

16

When limestone is older and smoother, it is not easy to see the shells. You can write on some kinds of limestone.

It takes many thousands of years to make limestone.

Limestone is used to make buildings.

Sandstone formations, Capitol Reef National Park, Utah

Sandstone is not always the same color.

Conglomerate is made underwater. It is made of little stones or pebbles held together by limestone.

Shale

Conglomerate

Shale is made underwater.
It is made of mud. It
smells muddy when it is
wet. It is many different
colors.

Shale scratches easily. It is not as hard as some other kinds of rocks. Find a piece of shale. Can you scratch it with a pin? Can you scratch it with a piece of glass? You probably will not be able to scratch some other rocks with a pin or a piece of glass.

Polished agate

Water helps make agate, too. Agate is harder than shale. It is not easily scratched. People polish agate and make things from it.

SOME ROCKS ARE MADE FROM OTHER ROCKS

Rocks that are made from other rocks are called metamorphic rocks. There are many kinds of metamorphic rocks. The heat of the earth and the weight of the many layers of rocks on top of rocks help them to change into different metamorphic rocks.

Slate in its natural setting that has been dug up by strip mining
at Terre Haute, Indiana

Slate is made from shale.

It is harder than shale. It will not scratch so easily.

Schist is made from conglomerate. It is many different colors.

Rare book library at Yale University is a granite
building with marble panels.

Marble is made from limestone. Marble is many different colors.

Marble can be made very smooth and shiny.

Gneiss may be made from granite. It has dark and light streaks in it.

ROCKS ARE MADE FROM MINERALS

There are many kinds of minerals in rocks. Some kinds of rocks have more than one mineral in them. Some kinds of rocks have only one mineral in them. Talc is a mineral.

A talc rock scratches very easily. You can scratch it with your fingernail. It feels smooth.

Quartz is a mineral. It is very hard. It is hard to scratch quartz—even with a knife.

Sometimes minerals are crystals. Crystals are clear and have a certain shape.

Quartz crystal, Brazil

Jewelry is often made of quartz crystals. Quartz crystals are sometimes called "clear ice."

Many kinds of rocks have quartz crystals in them. Granite has quartz in it.

Sometimes several crystals melt and harden into one piece. Then they are no longer crystals.

All these rocks are quartz. But not all of them are crystals.

Quartz

Sandstone has much quartz in it. Even little grains of sand are almost all quartz. Quartz sand makes good sandpaper.

Feldspar may be pink, green, or almost white.

Feldspar

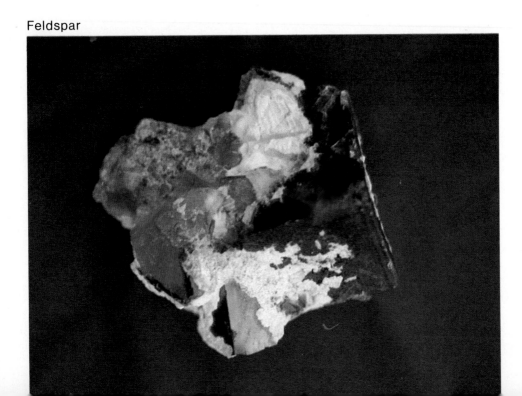

Feldspar crystals always have four sides. Not all feldspar is in crystals.

Calcite crystals make things look double. Not all calcite is in crystals.

Calcite crystals

Mica from North Carolina

Mica is made of many thin sheets. Some mica is black. Some is almost clear. It is easy to see through one of the clear sheets of mica.

It is easy to see the crystals in some kinds of rocks.

Red, gray, and white granite

Granite has crystals of quartz, feldspar, and mica in it. These crystals make granite look speckled.

Syenite looks very much like granite. This rock is not like granite because it does not have quartz in it.

ROCKS TELL STORIES OF LONG AGO

Some rocks have prints of plants or animals in them. The prints are called fossils.

It takes many thousands of years for a rock to be made.

The plants and animals that are pictured in rocks lived many thousands of years ago.

Fossils are usually found in limestone. This piece of limestone has a fossil of a fern in it.

This piece of limestone has a part of a fish in it. The fish part has turned to stone and is a fossil.

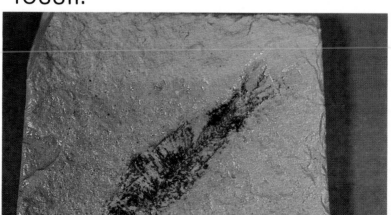

The rocks below have fossils of trilobites in them. Trilobite is the name given to an animal that lived long ago. No trilobites are alive now. We would not know about trilobites if there were no fossils in rocks.

Trilobites

Petrified Forest

Big pieces of trees
sometimes turn to rock. All
the little holes in the wood
fill in with minerals when it
turns to rock. Petrified
wood tells people where
big forests once were.

Limestone, Mississippi Palisades State Park

Layers of water-made
rock tell where seas once
covered the land.
It is fun to read the
story of our Earth in rocks.

SCIENTISTS NAME ROCKS

To find out about rocks, scientists do these things:

They break rocks open. They smell rocks when they are wet. They feel rocks. They scratch rocks to see how hard they are. They taste rocks. They test rocks with chemicals. They look at them through a magnifying glass.

Scientist examines a moon rock brought back to
Earth by *Apollo XIV.*

Scientists have given rocks names based on what they find out about them. Each rock in your collection should have a name. To learn about rocks and their names:

- look at them carefully,
- read about them in books,
- visit a museum,
- ask a scientist for help.

This book has told you about many kinds of rocks. Here are some of the things you know.

Rocks are different sizes and different colors.

Rocks are made in different ways.

Some rocks are made under the ground.

Above: Goblin Valley, Utah
Left: Arches National Park, Utah

Some rocks are made
above the ground.

Some rocks are made
underwater.

Rocks are being made
all the time.

Rocks are made of minerals.

Each kind of crystal has its own shape.

Some rocks are harder than others.

Some rocks are older than others.

Rocks tell stories of long ago.

Rock collection, mounted and identified

Rocks are useful.
There are many kinds of
rocks and it is fun to learn
about them.

WORDS YOU SHOULD KNOW

agate(AG • it) — a stone that is a type of quartz.

calcite(KAL • site) — a mineral which is in limestone, marble, and chalk.

chemical(KEM • ih • kil) — a substance made by or used in the study of other substances.

feldspar(FELD • spar) — a mineral found in igneous rocks.

foam(FOME) — a mass of tiny bubbles.

lens(LENZ) — an instrument that enlarges things; magnifier.

mica(MYE • kah) — a mineral that separates into thin layers.

mineral(MIN • er • il) — natural substances that make up rocks.

petrify(PET • rih • fye) — to turn wood or other material into stone.

speckle(SPEK • ill) — small bit.

syenite(SYE • en • ite) — a type of igneous rock.

trilobite(TRILL • oh • bite) — a small prehistoric animal

volcano(vol • KAY • noh) — an opening in the earth's crust through which lava, dust, and hot gases are thrown.

INDEX

About the author

Born and raised in western Iowa, Illa Podendorf has had experience teaching science at both elementary and high school levels. For many years she served as head of the Science Dept., Laboratory School, University of Chicago and is currently consultant on the series of True Books and author of many of them. A pioneer in creative teaching, she has been especially successful in working with the gifted child.